THE COMPLAINTS

T0345791

ALSO BY W. S. DI PIERO

Poetry

The First Hour
The Only Dangerous Thing
Early Light
The Dog Star
The Restorers
Shadows Burning
Skirts and Slacks
Brother Fire
Chinese Apples: New and Selected Poems
Nitro Nights
TOMBO

Essays

Memory and Enthusiasm: Essays 1975-1985
Out of Eden: Essays on Modern Art
Shooting the Works: On Poetry and Pictures
City Dog
When Can I See You Again: New Art Writings
Mickey Rourke and the Bluebird of Happiness: a Poet's Notebooks

Translations

Pensieri, by Giacomo Leopardi
This Strange Joy: Selected Poems of Sandro Penna
The Night of Shooting Stars: Selected Poems of Leonardo Sinisgalli
Ion, Euripides

THE COMPLAINTS

W. S. Di Piero

Carnegie Mellon University Press
Pittsburgh 2019

ACKNOWLEDGMENTS

The author thanks the following magazines where several poems in this book first appeared:

Kenyon Review: "In the Marina," "The Sidewalk Harvest"
New England Review: "The Family Circle"
Ploughshares: "Ash Wednesday on the 22-Fillmore Bus"
Plume: "Poems from Notebooks," "The Swallows," "Which Aisle?" "The Rain So Cold"
Poetry: "Lavender All Over Again"
Threepenny Review: "Wheels, Fenders, Windshields, Hoods," "Catch You at the Oregon," "The Words," "The Processionals," "By the Seawall," "At an Exhibition of Unfinished Works"
Zyzzyva: "The Young Alfonso," "Migrant Alfonso," "His Shadow Gets Away from Him"

Some of the poems appeared in a Plume Editions chapbook, *The Man on the Water*, published by MadHat Press.

Book design by Samantha Mack & Connie Amoroso

Library of Congress Control Number 2018955993
ISBN 978-0-88748-646-3

10 9 8 7 6 5 4 3 2 1

for Luca

CONTENTS

III

THESE EARLY FALL DAYS

I don't want wisdom, don't want the one
and every summed in potentate words
that parade on yellow leaves from gums
and ginkgos that shake their trashy skirts
to shiver color to this floor of things.
I don't want we. No choice oinker phrases.
I want the silver safety pin so bright
in that girl's lip, and seasonal silver
to foil the air like silver-leaf oaks
in their flush finalities. No ratiocination.

Butterscotch, lanolin, yes, agrodolce airs,
plasma, ores, recycling-bin realities,
troubled angels in posses on Market Street.

No conclusions from red leaves on grass and sidewalk,
from leaf-bits on my fingers and near noise that stitches
fall's debris falling down the towers of air.

THE PROCESSIONALS

Jet-lagged and a little drunk after *As Time Goes By* and other standards
in a rathskeller fake juke-joint in Florence, Christmas Eve, 1992,
I walked the piazza with other shades sliding across the walls,
the starless sky, the murderous palazzo, the timid Arno close
but quieted: on a stone bench, lovers mismatched in years held hands,
making an imperfect painful art of an impossible perfect one.
After dark, strangers and their sea-sound murmurs stir
in and out of lamplight. The postcard kiosk still burns bright.
We're inhaling gristly winter airs: past solstice, I feel slow
and fat with time, new time. Under the small cocky David,
two English bulldogs pull on a leash like monsters dragged
from underground by their lady's rhinestone purse and fox-head stole.
Herakles clubs the helpless Caco. Perseus lifts Medusa's orgasmic head.
Around such ecstasy of force a beautiful choral laughter rules
the airwaves around our heads. I'm at home in all this strangeness.
Hopeless Caco begs for deliverance. Cables drain from Medusa's head.
I hear them before I see them: saffron robes over union suits,
flip-flops, woolen socks, the Krishna initiates *chingching*-ing
like the tribe they were, emerging from the narrowest lane
where bulldogs, dame, kiosk, and I and others wait for them:
the bouncy slow procession timed to their finger chimes,
airy voices in happy adoration, unaware subversives
of our scene, a novelty act, a dancing gang of believers:
their shadows, too, walked across the walls in eggnog light,
then drifted down another lane. There and gone, like that,
like us, strangers to places, at home there, the music
a sprint of time, a something joy, a salty aromatic bread.

THEIR WINTER SONGS

The cranes are singing their sad songs across
the Sacramento River's Prospect Slough,
as they flew over Dante's head in hell,
files of carnal souls condemned to live
a million million times their gorgeous sins
of loving lust and corrupted mind, crying
their eternal patterns of useless come and go.
Their whippy files sweep the air: they want
to catch sight of love's body in the Pilgrim,
who visits their pain just that one time. What songs
did they not really sing? Engines and tires whish
outside my steamy bus, its tender lovers
chewing sandwiches and pears. Above,
the cranes sing that love is a waving line
in motion, in the wind, composed or deranged,
a passage in passage, a dampened, staggered trill,
as if practicing to find their voice again
and sing more of the lost. They remind me
how love's blood rushes to weary memory.
Dante's souls go nowhere for all time.
We bone and tissue creatures stir up embers
of fiery wish, we sing our aggrieved lais
to one another, while the cranes white out
beyond the horizon's stormy, late-day fires.

AN EVENING OUTSIDE CEDAR CITY

The cut, its petroglyphs of snakes, spears,
elk, human body parts, and dominoes
whose likeness I'd once seen in a museum
("marking celestial rhythms, Mexico, 400 C.E.") . . .
Some kid tagged the rock: LUIS LOVES BECKY GOMEZ.
Before we got that far, we'd raced before a storm,
looking for the abandoned farmhouse, its dead tree
and spiked buds that were eagles, who parted
their black gates then elbowed into flight
from the shape of waiting we'd see on that stone.

This dissonant rhyming world we keep falling into.
Rain and gusts banged the car, we drove back to town
to see, once the weather wiped, mountain elk grazing
freeway slopes, as they did that same week every year.
A stranger's soft voice fell on us (*There!*) like the rain
starting to fall again, where they stretched their necks
to lip juniper berries, grand and with no thought,
watching us, as if we were there to be seen
by them. They left that day and haven't come back,
who knows why, and took their coherence with them.

THE SWALLOWS

For you, naturally, only for you
and your love of plain growing
sumptuous things, here now,
from that hysterical earnest florist
on Via Ugo Bassi near Burger King,
rowdy debonair ranunculi for you.
Signor Histerica Passio declared,
Ranuncoli olandesi! Importantissimo,
somehow, the Holland angle
we teased out through dinner,
those knobby blackred blooms
I carried in my fist, as instructed,
upside down, to drain their biojuices
into stems, pistils, bloom-tissue,
as if to bait a grasping underworld,
to enliven and keep them fresh
the two smart blocks to your address,
where we set them on the terrace,
in a clay vase, between us and
our forty-year friendship. "We live
more than one life, we live a few,
they come and go, one and one,
we come and go, this life to that."
The city's inflamed roof tiles cooled
below us in the twilight sky:
the sulfur streetlamps pinked
Via dell'Inferno's cobblestones.
The watchful flowers darkened, too,
as we darkened, beside the rosemary
and gardenias, the soil stink insidious
among those aroused sweet scents,
while above us (remember?) around
the two ancient towers, the swallows
chased and fled their own whistling.

(for Cicci)

MONTALE'S MOTET #6
("LA SPERANZA DI PURE RIVEDERTI")

I was lost to the loss of hope
that I'd ever see you again

and wondered if
the scrim of images
you make of yourself
is a sort of death preview.
Or if it is, really, a glimpse,
after all this time, of you,
swift and migratory,
(in Modena, under the porticoes, a houseboy
in cockamamie livery
walked two jackals on a leash).

AT AN EXHIBITION OF UNFINISHED WORKS

The baby's see-through hand seeks out
the Virgin Mary's cheesecloth breast
that ripens bluely toward his mouth.

A noble's chalky fingers crawl from
his velvet cuffs: they point to a roughed-out,
rock-candy skull, as if to instruct us

this is ours, this country of the real,
its constant coming into form and going.
The girl on the trapeze yearns toward

the catch, sees all that unpainted space,
stretching to complete the sexual act.
It doesn't end, the flight, the save.

My hand rests on the bench still warm
from another's presence. My skin's
crosshatched, thin, webbed with age,

and yet the air feels like fine fire
laid to leave a small story there
that's waiting for its proper end.

IN THE MARINA

It squeezes the spleen
this sunny winter's
New Year's morning,
not the pain itself
but the too much of it,
the inexcusable with
its perfect right to exist,
the grass shining bright
along Marina Green,
the tipping masts,
the small tide that raps
piers and rolling hulls
creaking, while you weep
harder into the cold wind:
your hot pain loves this
anniversary of his death
the wind carries through
your loud red blouse,
broken hoarse voice,
and flighty hands
the wind can't calm.
Kiddies wrangle their bikes
through our promenade,
elders, us, dogs, him,
lovers on their elbows
on all this perfumed grass,
so why not cry out for what's
not here and the too much
that walks along with it?

THE MAN ON THE WATER

December's wind jerks spindrift puppets
down Chicago's River: they flee the water
they're made from, they wade in it, walk on it,

they inflate into hourglass coils that spray
into nothing and collapse while he's rigged,
two streets over, to IVs in the chemo room.

The crocus will pop, the forsythia shake its yellow.
It's hard to think of the sparings of spring.
I've never felt so hurt by hard, blown cold.

The crows, our wise brothers, beat against
the feathered grains that populate the river.
Michigan Ave., late morning, the ironwork bridge:

I should see his diminished form gray and fugitive
upon the water. I don't. The wind blows too hard.
Rude Chicago how beautiful you are your mukluks

parkas mittens mufflers. Hardly anybody's here.
Where did they all go? The cancer's in blood and bone.
The bitterness slows me. The wind licks scratches

on my face not my face. In October he'd been all
bones and scraped skin, four weeks in hospital,
home for Halloween, when the twins kicked up

the tumbling cereal leaves and slapped at them.
An ice-cream cart beeped through charred air.
The trick-or-treaters dragged or swung big bags.

I felt the gentle gusts create more time around us.
A neighbor's spring-loaded pop-up whiskered ghoul
sensed our presence and arose from its stubble yard.

We forget too much. In an hour I'll pick him up.
Next day, the girls screamed and cried when we passed
the dormant cobwebbed thing that once greeted us.

ONE AND TWO AND THREE

The junco's black crown
twitched on its even
blacker branch that dipped
after the bird was gone—
my fingers grabbed
at almond blossoms
the wind plucked
and threw past bees.
So that's one. That's me.

Two is you, nervous,
combing out your hair,
bright loose long,
stroked to the zippy glides
of juncos, bees, wind,
leaning to one side
flecked by white petals
from the rocking branch
where the bird just was.

And here you are again,
thought up, thought back,
person become the poem
in this unreal time
while morning foglight
breaks behind your wrists
that still shake long-lost
fleshy white phosphors
from your slight hands.

"PACIFIC SURFLINER" NOW ARRIVING SAN DIEGO

Everybody's here. Cowboys, Mennonites, Tijuana illegals,
Muslim cabbies at prayer on loading docks as dark clouds
fuss above a southerly sun past its prime. In the Depot's
Moorish architecture of displacement, squeaky kids
trawl satchels through the shed, their happy voices
mystically far from home. The waiting room's tiled light
anoints life lived imperfectly here or somewhere else.

Killing time, my life mostly miscues and hesitance,
I want something to take me over, so I look around
the baggage claim for you, who could have been
anybody from anywhere, like Ellis Island's ghosts,
their dump of cardboard valises, bindles, baby-fat sacks
strangled by hemp. . . . Here are long-haul lovers,
roughnecks, girls in heels grabbing Samsonites.

It must be why I'm here, to wait and see who claims
what looks too much like your brown suede duffel bag
that "carries dead things well" inside its scuffed hide.
Nasal music threads the scene tonight while you weave
through music somewhere else. That bag and us—
the Garment District, two Venices, South End, South Philly,
scraped nap, brass hasps, gaunt warmed handle . . .

A teenage girl two hands it off the belt and waddles
into the runny sun, your bag five years late,
thumping fresh thighs and dimpled knees.
The voices thrill me. The engine horn is howling.
I smell hot-oil residues, and candy corn.
I've felt this way before, at home in time but lost.
Where are you now that you're near me again?

THE SIDEWALK HARVEST

They must be moving, maybe changing towns.
Here's the saw he sized their bedstead on,
and flatware, cheerful flattened beach balls,
throw rugs, highball glasses, steamer trunk.
It takes too many weeks to move. See them
punish their small rooms and obese garage
with an unloved silence they've somehow learned
they can't live without: and out from that silence
they gently drop aggrieved, pale, sincere words
into the children's hair, who hardly hear.

He used to balance on this gimpy ladder,
and with these hard-caked gloves rake sodden leaves
from sagging gutters that engorged and poured
shredded sheets of winter rain outside
their ashy windows. She wept in reckless spring
over her chives and holy basil that he
chopped and dropped in restless stews and soups
that simmered in these earnest pans now stacked
like tipsy chapeaus with no party to attend.
Passing cars slow down to view the goods.

Where will they go, the opaline lampshade
and stopped clocks and diamond paste,
while he and she won't anymore be telling
how the day went, who called, what kiddo did.
And don't forget the comforter, those stains
that we deposited like essences.
Remember us then? We thought we were
plummy immigrants so fresh to life
and anything strange. Desirous, too,
though what we desired we could not tell.

Bright strangers to this dimmed imperium
now pull up, ask our best price for blender,
unfinished quilt, broke rocker and broke books
and faulty shelves, the drop-leaf table, the dresser,
and bed-frame parts I planned out and true-cut
as a kit we'd break down then rejoin
whenever we made our next big move
and reclaimed our lives, our unconscious days—
the kit would make it all much simpler when
we lay in one another's arms, told stories, and slept.

WHICH AISLE?

I'm making Lady Hardware sad.
She's noble in her fuschia smock
and grayed, pinned-up hair, and loves
the title I've conferred on her.
She's bummed because today I bring,
broken from a neighbor's tree,
sprigs of the life of western things,
the labials of mock-oranges,
such dirty trees, but I don't care,
because they're the end of the world.
I offer them to her large nose,
she shuts her eyes, she's in Eden.
No. No. "Yes I can," I say and sing
"I certainly can can-can,"
anything to lighten our mood,
because she can tell how lost I am
to my errand's hopelessness.
"I want this, I have to have this
in my apartment." *No way, big boy.*

When I came here in the seventies,
its scent hid inside fog, car lights,
wet winds, fire sirens, pork buns,
I carried it in my nose, on my skin,
I smelled it whenever I chose, I want
all that impacted time and place
with me as these small days run down,
let me keep it, preserve it somehow,
freeze or cork or atomize
the citrusy humid ga-ga drift
that calls back insane florid sex
and hurts my forehead when I inhale.
In an apartment, not a chance,
I'm sorry, honey, but give it up.
She doesn't say: You fool, you,
who doesn't carry lost things?
You're a strange child for a man your age,
but an old man is bound to be a little
off and gone. The rage comes naturally.

"LAVENDER ALL OVER AGAIN"

Newspaper caption

I see you in your backyard's lavender,
post-lunch doze, dreaming some boy-star
you brought home last week who blurs
to hummingbirds that fan your ears.
Lavender buds pilled your sweatshirt
in the restaurant garden you preferred,
where we ate, gossiped, laughed,
and drank a half-liter carafe.

You ate experience whole,
sweetest when you lost control.
I see you spring from sleep:
bright fog rolls toward your seat.
You partied hard way past your prime.
Give me wine wine all the time time.
Ardent life burned in your heart and hands.
You took the heat till you could barely stand.

(Thom Gunn: 1929-2004)

WHEELS, FENDERS, WINDSHIELDS, HOODS

It tasted bitter, burnt, like most things that summer,
the medicinal orange-peel darkness in the shot glass,
the day's damp heavy veils forming around the sun,
around groggy lumps in work boots opening car doors,
while she, at 5 a.m., in her silence and widowed blacks
sat across from me and my young, stupid years.
Her mottled hands showed me what was what:
a Fernet shot, butter brimming the toast,
raw eggs I sucked from rococo old-country cups,
biscotti to dunk in bitter coffee—they'd bear me
like the man I might become, through the dark
to work the line at Ford's Pennsauken Depot.
I hardly knew her, my grandmother's sister,
but took her tomato-and-mayo sandwiches
on hot close rides with men in white T-shirts
who rolled the windows down and smoked or snored.
Lunchtime, lying inside shipping crates we built
along the line, picking and loading stock, I read
our defective Catholics, *Dubliners*, *Brighton Rock*,
their sentences like foreign languages or chants
or calls. And magnanimous Whitman, Durrell
and his olive trees, and beautiful broken Delmore,
how I loved him, he was educated, he could sing—
Time is the fire in which we burn. I was myself
a squealing snotnose rhapsody, reading on breaks:
I wanted out, a world elsewhere, no more dialects
and hoagies, alley fights and fake florals,
women's voices ripping space to rags,
pasty summers, packing grease, and Tastykakes.
After work, back from Jersey, the light softened
South Philly's brick and glass. Paul Klee said to me:
a drawing is taking a line for a walk, so take it
for a walk that becomes a sentence in lines.
Neighbors on front steps, transistors, the pretzel guy
banging his bell, and Good Humor's pathetic tinkle.
No music or TV inside her house of shades.
I spent those summer hours, one year short
of getting out, finally, reading for my life
in her son's room. She didn't talk about it,
the secret they all observed: curtains drawn,

she sat and crocheted the Sacred Heart,
while Nico, Angelo, Tino, whatever his name was,
abided absent from her parlor: while upstairs
I heeded voices, the long gone son chain-smoked,
serving time, doing eternal push-ups
in Eastern State Penitentiary, a murder charge,
who he killed I never knew. She sat heavily
in the burnt-almond dark of her house undelivered
from all that, the misbegotten, the unforgiven,
time embittered by time. That summer before I left
the village life that reared me and put ashes
in my mouth and anger in my stifled wild heart,
I lodged in his room, ate raw eggs, got angrier,
hungrier for words in smart disturbing orders:
Zi' Mari' saw me off to work, where we hid crickets,
from the unassembled crates stored outdoors,
inside our foreman's desk, what a prick,
he pushed the line to ace his Christmas bonus,
Shorty Boyle was his name, I curse him forever here,
our crickets made him flap his lips and blubber,
mockery of the water world, uglier than catfish
that filled The Lakes, where only black folks fished.
I can say here the impossible, the silly, the true.
Who's listening? Zi' Mari', when did you die?
Old sorrowful woman, your son is still upstairs,
you hardly spoke a word, I speak back to you now,
and serve you this, my dear, in the near dark.

THE FAMILY CIRCLE

1. *Somebody Say Grace*

Here we are again, Friday night
in that Watkins Street kitchen
with our serious friend, Silence,
and her clenched, unpleasant cousins,
Fault and Grievance. I'm the child,
so they must love me. Pop gets tripe
stewed in red sauce and beer.
The tripe forgives his few brown teeth.
Dad's dazed and grim before his slice
of fried boloney, his boiled beets,
the merry meatballs of last week
a sorry memory now: they'll reconvene
upon the oilcloth some day soon.
What can our dago family say
on its way to America, to sweet corn
and true chocolate, where the TV set
gasses the house with eager voices?
Nobody talks much in America
at this table, still shipping on its way
to America. Pop cranks his tongue,
Dad starts to cry. But why? Who knows?
And Mom indicts the poor potatoes
she pokes and sticks with an angry fork.
Here it is that we remain, at this board,
uttering aspirations, giving thanks
for what we're not and won't soon be.

2. *The Aspirations*

They aren't seeking anything. They want.
They don't know what they want.
So here they are as usual, their boy,
devoutly short of breath, on his knees,
dog-face earnest, while across from Dad
mother's ruby nails pinch her rosary
toward pain, and her husband studies
a dark floor that must look far away.
Their boy after supper leads them
around aspirations he's memorized.
He aspires to he knows not what,
Mother of God Have Mercy on Us,
you know what I mean? And also,
for Christ's sake, Sacred Heart of Jesus,
I was saying, save us sinners, now,
Merciful Mother Please Do Us Right.
And is Pop still alive? Dead? We *forgot?*
Hey ho the daffy boy leads them,
but they look weary and already old.
Mom won't let Dad forget it's two days
since he shaved, and has sister disappeared
into a wood? No woods in the neighborhood!
Ah, there she is, the little sister we forgot,
in finger curls and pinafore, who quakes
while the ejaculations purr around
the tight lost circle they compose.

EGYPT AT PEP'S

Now still here
as I was then
the somber child
in a car window
observing pigeons
flying sideways
through great buildings
and grand cricket
fire escapes:
and the syph
we ridiculed
hitch-stepping past
Voodoo Lou's
shrunken-head shop
down South Street
near neon Pep's
where Yusef Lateef
wailed mizmar snake-
charming songs:
I still haven't
passed them by,
they didn't pass me,
these all-my-life
laminated sheets
wrapped opaque
around my heart;
the hours didn't go
anywhere but here,
pressing harder by
the day, the days.
Outside Pep's
I'm here down
my newest street:
I tell myself to sing,
sing things austere and vast
as magic lantern panes.
The ravens mind
the chimney pots,
and over on Fillmore,
where Rasselas folded,

the CD vendor
stands his corner,
though the flugelhorns
trombones vibes
have left the clubs
for concert halls.
Abstraction has
its sheer beauty
but diminishes us,
while a ripe banjoist
somewhere down
some other street
sings "Roxanne."

MARIA ANGELUCCI

She laughs before the word occurs to her.
They *pop* into her brain, she says, like *popcorn*,
her village words from forty years ago,
out from steerage, giving her the giggles.
At first, few came, her unexpected guests,
but then brought their whole damn families.
Useless words for "ashtray" and "goat" arrived.
The older she got, the more words entered her house.
One day the plumber gave her a look when,
explaining to him what broke, she popped into
correct Italian for "pipe," "tap," "turn off."
See what I mean, she said, the years I spent
learning English, what happens? Down the drain.
The plumber shrugged. Lady, if you don't mind.

CATCH YOU AT THE OREGON

Steam finagled your hair, the amber shades clouded
behind the coffee lines you blew across the cup—
you sipped and tuned things out, the world can wait.
That was this time last year. I just fell into it again.
You seemed to be watching us be there, or observing
some other history. The scene had no meaning,
it was an ordinary decorated moment,
the shades, your head, circus-hoop earrings, steam,
but I'd dropped into the cylinder where events toss
with others from other times and make a noise:
one of the restored F-line trolleys sledded past,
Robin Hood-green streamlined by a sharp red stripe,
the same one I'm sure I rode in 1956, down 9th Street,
past Horn and Hardart's baloney and lemon meringue:
Eisenhower's pruney face on the morning news,
after jerky images of Budapest, said the United States
shall not intervene: Old World streets, broken bottles,
smoke, rocks, rags, college kids, even girls in skirts,
threw bricks and stood in the path of Russian tanks.
Gangrenous politics never meet our need for sense,
the world's force can't be transformed to grace,
the conviction that the world defeats us rose
like a sickness of unreason in the childish me.
What our innocent diner scene reminded me of,
when that trolley went past, wasn't just Ike's
tweedy black-and-white TV moment, one more
storm of a moment, any moment in bloody time:
that trolley I was talking about terminated
near the stainless-jacketed Oregon Diner,
its ashtrays, linoleum, hot roast beef sandwiches,
where we boys, years past Budapest, in our useless
sexed-up chaos, finished our famished nights.
I remember mostly not the coffee but the steam,
how it seeped from everything, though I know
that can't be so, from urns, grill, menus, jukebox,
and the high hair of our pudgy waitress, Fran.
By then late night news in living color flashed
different faraway wars and their dead kids.
Where are you now? You with your buggy shades
who never rode an historic trolley car till now
I say it's so. I'm still here across from you.
Weird grainy steam hangs in the air of things.

TO SFO

The nude, a naked woman,
materializes in a condo window:
her houselights expand the frame
he now steps into, dressed to go,

like me, at 5:30 a.m., on my way
among the cabs and headlights and reds
in their blasted speedway corridors.
The moonlight spanks the waters.

The come and go of local life fills me
with sadness. Time hurts. Where am I?
(Rt. 101 S, out of San Francisco.) Where
am I going? (Newark, then New York

and its peoples.) The terminal's noise
sirens weird silence. On the Jetway,
we all pretend we're not about to rise
into the heavens that once were there.

Soon I'll be fearless among best sellers,
jaunty screens, stale feet, cold fries,
gorilla backpacks, Blake's screeching babes
bounced by parents in cargo pants . . .

Our diverse unrest confers on me
an obliging calm and aggrieved patience.
The nude in the window stays with me,
and the moment of her man, inviolable,

steady in mind, a momentous ordinary,
as I fly between a grape sweatshirt
who tanked in Reno, and she who walked
unhappily from her still good marriage.

THE RAIN SO COLD

The air of the day abhors us
and drives outliers like her
inside the crowded train.
She speed talks *it hurts*
my eyes it's too wet
like wet whatever
and cold in my eyes.
I ride the length of town
with her and smiling nuns,
skateboards, teens kissing,
toddlers on leashes,
Mission Bay to Ocean Beach.
Wet riders come and go.
The orator and I hold firm.
Who gives alms to Poor Tom
when the foul fiend vexes?
The rain lets up:
out on the sidewalks
Asian gleaners appear
with smiley-face latex gloves
and XXL garbage bags,
neatly dressed, picking through
the city's sinuses,
fastidious and focused
among the street singers
and their pussy scabs split
across raw fatty hands:
they sing to their doubles,
the elementals and invisibles
whose squeaky vocals reel
from tree roots and concrete.

JACKSON POLLOCK LINES

("I am nature.")

Three days' rain
        mars oak leaves,
writes mud blueblack
        on pavements,
pills the willowy dust
        on my window.

A million ants
        harvesting larvae
drain like rainwater
        down tree bark.
My God burns quiet
        in their quick stream.

A DAY IN THE COUNTRY

The country of contingency
is full of rain. From the gray hills
disappearing in the drizzly fog
yesterday's slow, capable stream
flows faster now, as if aimed
at those on the riverbank
it soon will breach, where they
have come to wade, the father
squatting there, hand-panning
pebbles and making marks
in the mud, talking to himself,
while the mother can be heard
among the trees, laughing at them,
at the trees, the larch trees,
scolding them for their color,
so contrary, quickened, heavenly.
Where have the children gone?
Here we are, watching it all,
hidden among the upland firs,
hiding from each other and from
that diluvial world down there.
The rain that falls on them
won't fall on us, who watch
from our unserious high ground
and cover ourselves with leaves,
like embers waiting for morning
and this bad weather to break.

WORDS FOR NIMROD

The more excellent their trade before they built the tower,
the more rough and barbarous became their speech now.

De Vulgari Eloquentia

My stonecutters honked.
Hod carriers *kree*-ed like hawks.
Carters clucked like barnyard fowl.
We built something to last.

Master planner, swinish me.
Great things we had to say got left
unsaid. Quitting time came fast.
But what we built still stands.

You still scream its use at it.
Tell this to you and your kind,
who think your politic words
will unify and save you.

RAVEN HAS HIS SAY

Ratso pigeons!
Strictly for the birds!

Morning vocalizing
settles one's nerves.

Practice makes perfect.
Hello high wire art!

O, come back, you
red-tail youth. Upstart.

Hair bulbs down there.
Taste, feed, need.

Sunshine so justified
upon my wings while

I sing for my supper.
Puppy litter. Woof.

Kittykats. Chickees.
Big Chief Sky-King me.

Red-tail now
agh! family-size.

Bring it on! My heart's
of stone-gold carved.

Big Bad Hey-Hey
of Plumage Ebony,

way back in the day
I was already me.

POEMS FROM NOTEBOOKS

In the Kitchen

We talk about how
       our words seem
to come between us.
      The paring knife slips,
slices a thumbnail,
       garlic half-moons fall,
blood arcs on the bamboo,
       lightning lights up
the dark broken sky
       and shocks the asphalt shingles,
we chase the lightning down
       by talking faster.

★★

He Says She Says

Love, sex love I mean, is predatory.
         That's what we're born and meant for.
         It's never nice. Desire eats us up
           and we eat it up and never finish.

          Kittiwake, kingfisher, kite,
       a magpie's blacks and whites
    on blacktop in the redwoods.
Do you see what I see?

★★

Mackerel in the Sea

are in the sky where they look like
                    the sandy ribs the tide has left behind,
and farther out the sea's oiled surface is
                    a mackerel skin the sun loves to lick.
Here along my streets are mackerel scales
                    of rain and lights that stripe the air:
the fog detests their sharper edges,
                    the winter cold eats them up.
The candlelight inside the rain that streaks the window
                    holds mackerel schooling out at sea.

★★

The Settlements

My cab driver can't shut up
about all this silly self stuff,
who needs it when you believe?
You pray, the voice of God
will be there for us but
life is life anyway, yes?
He left wife and kids behind
in Palestine, ten years now,
money for them, I need money,
a kidney transplant, shoes, teeth,
pray for me, my friend,
because He meant for you
to be here, to pray for me.

★★

On the Radio

The musician from Mali
plucks his kora, picks at
our nerves, the strings
run through navel to groin
to heel and toe as if
the body could lift itself
out of body even while
the sound wires itself
deeper than we've gone
inside our own selves:
its hairy roots push down,
grip tighter inside us,
reaching for darker water
running underground.

★★

To Joan Miró, db, Billie Miró, Thelonius Blue, and a Certain Friends

Fins and feathers.
Bowels and blood.
Our night sky blued,
its star-buds and lures
and black banana boat
and constellation of fish
fornicating a cloud,
its kite of a red moon-
scythe now the face
that is a sandy hill.
Pubes and pups.
Teardrops and tracks.

★★

The Time of Day

They are inspiration without purpose,
the cut shades of ravens in the sun,
under the sun, in morning's tender light.

They sail and shrink across tarred roofs,
their black now blacker sailing there,
the flight of shadows that cannot fly,

an astonishment on the wing of the air,
shades of no underworld that go in search
of shadows they do not know the shapes of yet.

★★

The Feel of Things

We live into the pauses, love,
and the places we've left behind
coat our bodies as if with
cobwebbed air or foam that
we feel faithful and tickly,
somehow even taste
on each other's flesh
but can't clearly see.

★★

And Just Like That

like sea swimmers
   shaking their violent hair,
the city cypresses
   from the cold tips
of their tough needles
   shake loose in the wind
black brittle drops
   that prickle the night air,
lit inside by ardent
   bearded streetlamps.

★★

The Motion

The ravens roust the red-tail,
its redness fills and flails the window,
the sun barks their smart blackness

and cut-outs houses, backyards—
the sun that moves around us
while we move around its fires.

THE WORDS

When they were young, tender-tough, exposed,
desiring experience but not knowing they desired,
words lived in small dense neighborhoods as sounds
without meaning, but street smarts shaped them
into a kind of plainsong that in time cried itself
into language, a pond-scum shape of sentences,
dragonflies, red dragonflies, and toads and reeds,
the longer the sentences, the more the words
wished for and wanted to claim, the more they felt
like stuff, like honeycomb and hair combs,
billy clubs, skinks, cardboard, silks, and concrete,
and soon became the things they said they were,
they imagined living other lives as other things,
like red rivets on bridge towers and the photons
glinting there, or crushed oyster shell and the drive
they cover in some bayou parish, in time the words
became one mind that owned it all, that lived
as if it could be alive with all things all at once,
a dreamed-up city crying sweet throaty noise,
but soon they became lowdown, slutty with desire,
derelict, living off the streets, begging small change,
attaching themselves there, here, and our words,
just like that, become us, they are what we have
and yet still want so badly that it hurts.

BEFORE THE READING

Plattsburg's Phantom F-4s wilded the atmosphere.
It started to drizzle. My host rushed me to see
Dannemora's main street, its forty-foot-high white wall,
TV news dishes idled outside like seers
awaiting signs. The jets broke above like storms.
"A poet has to see it, walk the wall." But I don't look
for subjects; the wall's just a dreadful stupid thing,
a mass-grave marker, a policy. The planes went home.

The rains blew hard and flapped their meaty wings,
pounding down the jets' too-silent aftermath.
Now we drove faster, to meet his writer friend,
who lived in a house beside a small stream in flood.
The waters ran too close. Deeper, inside the house,
an angry woman and a babe in arms cried out
to river and to husband. I couldn't understand.
"We have to go. It's no great loss. We're running late."

I tell myself to make words be the pith and bark
that experience is, not abstracted from it.
Aspiration loves impossibility.
The men aren't behind the wall, they're inside it,
set into whitewash and concrete. The wall is them
silenced, killing time. Forty years ago,
the cries inside that house were like the river's voice.
I don't remember the names. That night I ran late.

SATURDAY AND ITS AUTUMN WIND

My yearning is a steady stretched constant burn that beats not for
but toward something, pining forward, heady, consuming even
memory's helpless dear inventions. It's aroused in the catch-up
of a moment. It comes, I'm unaware, unprepared, I bear it
into the world, it's a new necessity, like the old ones. I yearn for
the wooly slash of sunlight, late afternoon, falling on my old address,
Strada Maggiore 6, as so many stanchions staffs poles of light fall through
Bologna's porticoes: it looks like a flaw in the camera lens,
made not by fact and memory but by defect. Life thrives on error.
"Flawed learning," your phrase, yes, a mistake already that might hurt us.
A state of the heart, of the nerves, yearning's pain feels good.
As I lie here, a breeze comes gusting through the window,
my head close enough to hear the zephyr-y hush as if it were
the breath of one of my dear dead combing through my hair.
I'm reading about the failing forgetful mind "beginning to slide away
from the adhesive friction that makes an individual possible."
The wind is unforgiving. What doesn't form and dissolve
sometime somewhere? I know the lost will call to me. I wake
with a surging ache of impossible return. There was
the one-time-only *tumpf* when the batter punched a softball
and the infield's extreme green brightened to bursting as if by force
of that comic *tumpf*: such green, I yearn for it, it won't occur again,
like the stringy knot of hair you left last night between the pillows,
your "love's tangles lost" that I yearn to touch right now.

(for GLS)

EL NIÑO

My windows buck in winds that shear
off the blue moon's ocean. Poetry can't
redeem the time, cellular time, the planet.
Ends and means concentrate in us.
The rain swipes and pats the glass.

I watch the world's atomic force,
the mindless beauty of what happens.
The stringy hair of pepper trees, jasmine,
camphors. Name them. They beat in time,
back and forth, as if impatient with their lives.

Irregularity is the utmost pattern.
It thrills and menaces, shuts airports,
floods streets, rumbles my room.
I'll wake tomorrow and still feel how
it shakes the mind of my heart.

THE COMPLAINTS

1. The Young Alfonso

We said he rolled in horseshit. His luck
never failed. He smelled pristine
like rose sachets his mother bought
to freshen drawers. He rolled and rolled,
never broke an ulna when we skated,
polio passed him by, no pink eye,
his fingers and toes grew straight.
We treated him so tenderly.
Lend out his preservative blessing
he could not do, but we kept him close.
His friend horseshit was everywhere:
its gold flakes scaled off steaming piles
that stunk to God in heaven before they dried:
fruit monger, cop, givella water man,
their horses dropped vegetal coals,
the sun's confetti. He had no power to heal,
to stop the blue storms that blew ticks
down our street but brought no luck
to anybody else. He had perfect skin.
Like any aloof, self-centered saint,
he lacked good sense and like a girl
talked fast, squealy, and too much.
He moved away, we knew not when but knew
he took with him his awful gift:
our fortunes got blasted, anyways,
by crass circumstance, the gods as ever
ungood and unambiguous toward us.

2. Migrant Alfonso

The city streets were good to me.
I felt watched over. Houses here
chop up and down the verdant hills
like auspicious Monopoly hotels.
The streets scrubbed and vacant,
topiary shaved into chess pawns,
chipmunks, hearts. I miss the baroque
manure altars that sanctified
my neighborhood. The suburbs worship
many gods, none true. I get into fights
in lots where houses just like ours
will go, box by cretinous box.
I broke a knuckle and ruined a shirt.
Pain justifies me here. Affliction feels
like good, dirty, deserved grace.
Broken home, broken blessing:
a 7-Eleven cop picked up Dad
for vagrancy. He wanted, he said,
to keep close to me and his bike
and "kissing distance" to Mom.
Jesus don't walk with me here.
I miss my horseshit dispensation:
my body slid through the pasty air
like a shape of purpose in motion.
Our subdivision's bellicose newness
crapped my old luck. Now am I sick
with alien agues, cankers, zits
sans physic. My body's a migraine,
a shadow me of unauthored pains,
sleepwalking, goofed-up, at a loss.

3. His Shadow Gets Away from Him

I watched my shadow flee to find
its way alone. It jumped the moon
in a puddle by a curb and leaped
its greasy shadow leaping there.

It climbed a house and curtained down
upon a family of flesh-stalks gathered
by an almond tree, talking politics.
It eavesdropped on the uselessness.

I let it gleefully go as if it were
a thing of the past, its fortunes shot,
or a prayer or hymn or curse I left
in church or at the farmer's market,

where plums and pomegranates shine:
go, my shadow, and unbenison them.
I'm glad to live without you. Fasten not
your drear promise to me again.

4. These Jersey Sheets from Jersey

I watched a sleepy boy on Sunday,
still in his icy blue pajamas,
revolve inside the sudsy washer
with sheets and sleeping bags.
I think his mother left him there.

His face dissolves inside the drum.
He's jellyfish, kelp, manatee, foam.
He must be having fun. He rubs his face
against the glass, this squirmy boy
I was. To live past childhood

was such a dreary effort, outside
the drum, lost as I was to images
draining in my head. I feared the world.
It hurt to live in it unmothered.
The tumbling boy is safe, couched, slow.

★

Hey, lover girl, I tried to clear the sheet's
semen lube sweat pinkish blood and wine
we tasted on pluvial March nights:
amethyst sheets from Hackensack that chafed
before we broke them in. That really was

my marbled face behind the door,
the rinse cycle revenant who won't
give up. Amethyst, your stone, charm
against pain poison mischance loss,
against my dream life's catastrophes.

To sleep in one another's arms,
heedless of loss yet turbulent
with dreams of your blue parakeets
in catacombs, your daddy costumed
in his coffin as the Queen of Hearts.

*

Black boys in my neighborhood,
who never crossed into our streets,
begged house to house, Halloween's
dispensation, in old-man overcoats,
corked faces, and nylon stocking caps.

Did I tell you that? What else to say?
We animals long to be together in
an instant of out-of-time time while in
this quickened riddled here and now.
The ceiling fans will cool us down.

The voices inside the wall must be
that couple arguing.Someone left
big boisterous flowers in the hall.
Why do we feel as if the flowers
are filling up with trembling us?

5. The Motion Pictures

That winter in Vienna, the Ferris wheel gondolas rose
into the chilly grays. I chewed warm chestnuts from
wax paper like the kind mom wrapped sandwiches in
for weekend matinees. Tomatoes soaked the bread
and squirted on my tongue. Harry Lime, up there,
in a godly mood, recites his chippy, knowing lines
about the Swiss, their cuckoo clocks, the Renaissance,
the silly dots down below. Those dots were us.
The plane tree leaves cracked underfoot. Alida Valli
walks at us in the final shot and kicks through leaves
of fallen souls. She'd always love Harry. I knew it.
"The Third Man" played at Germantown's Bandbox:
from zebra-striped seats I watched a carnival mob
engulf the mute clown Batiste: his silence gave
such helpless life to me. Our own great clown's a Jew:
Elliot Gould tooted his baby harmonica,
"Hooray for Hollywood" crashed the soundtrack
to his loopy dance under trees, *The Long Goodbye,*
Milan, 1973, a dubbed print. International me.
I'd seen America and Europe at the North Point,
Bullitt's Mustang, *Straw Dogs'* mantrap, *Pierrot le Fou's*
obese Gitanes, *The Piano Player's* bloody snow.
The pictures leave nothing to chance. I wanted that
second life to make me free. In *The Conformist,*
Marcello finds, in a rent-boy's crib, still alive,
the childhood driver he thought he'd killed.
The light flickers shapeless forms on walls and floors.
Like one of Plato's shutaways, Marcello turns and looks
through the fire at us. The world is still far away.
I tasted tomatoes, smelled mustardy upholstery,
saw Harry's shadow batwing through the sewers,
Harry the final fool, who believed he had every right.

6. My Fats

The Beatles came to Point Breeze Avenue
to meet the man. That's where Fats Domino lived.
I thought I was the only diehard fan
who knew the truth. I knew he really lived
in New Orleans. I didn't care. I'd drop off
a re-heel job at Jocko's Shoe Repair,
and there he was, the grin, the flat-top conk,
my homegrown ringer for the grand Fat Man.
"Poor Me" cranked from his mini-Magnavox
across to The Breeze and its matinee awards,
the gildered cups and plates and H-I-G
encyclopedia volume that left off there.
Next door, tripe and oxtails hung from hooks.
Nylons and garters posed in Hansen's window.
The American heart eats itself. What music
do we make? Our president's a screechy fool.
Black boys came my way, it was their street,
I grabbed the soda bottle of my errands
but wasn't jumped, not that time. It was as good
as having Fats among us, and when the Beatles
found him in New Orleans and jammed, my Jocko
comped with them, he had a great left hand
and rocked, eyes closed, busted shoes around him.
I got lucky that day. Nobody knew
I was the only one who heard them play.

7. Here We Go Again at 4 A.M.

My body is fortune's furnace.
My brain's coral coals gash
and fall into my joins and seams.

I'm a pelican. My heavy skull bombs
into the marsh, to put the fire out.
God leaves no thing unburned.

Pain's a bitch in heat, hot, hot,
historical. The sun suffers
up into my throat each day.

Pain's a babe who plays with matches.
My knuckles grind. The day is just
getting started. Its fires light up

raspy brasses, oboes, bassoons,
comic-fierce, Ives, Bartok, O
my fire fathers, noising through these bones.

8. I Keep Your Time

The breath you draw
and stop, not near the top.

Come home soon, love.
The dust motes miss you.

I still haven't finished
touching up the trim.

I measure the hours till
they're all used up.

Your photo-booth card
From Sassy Tallahassee,

badly overexposed,
closer to the ghost:

you in gloves and hat,
seated on the chair,

glassy, milky, vague,
your perishable self's

nearly erased hands,
bonnet ribbon, and frill.

9. My Two Sleeps

Between my first and second sleep,
stars looked impoverished in my window.
I made coffee and watched the streets.
In my first, I'd been sick, laid low

in dreams of melancholy, ablaze
with guilt for melancholy's sorrow.
I was a poor dim world dispraised:
a purple bloodstain marked my brow.

Between my first and second sleep,
my book told me this: love and wrath,
hope, faith, and jealousy enchant
life's rank unreasonable path.

I'm a believer. I know how to wait.
The window ran with winter rain
that infuriated and tapped my pulse.
Rain said: worlds change and change.

In my second sleep, I didn't dream.
When I woke I had a memory
of being free, somehow: it seemed
too real. I'd blended with the sky.

After my two faint sleeps, I felt
I'd lost a week. O my stardust,
carbon soul, time's an insult,
a grievance given to us, in trust.

Between my first and second sleep,
I write lines to delay the day, to calm
my spirit tantrums, weep, or tweak
desires that still sing me like psalms.

10. Ash Wednesday on the 22-Fillmore Bus

Plow your tweener backpack
into your fellow sinner.
I was fallen, too.

Sulk into your years
and cropped organdy nails.
Everybody's watching.

Your body's burnt to ash,
to the stranger's thumbprint
on your stubborn pimples.

I see a younger you,
the candle-smoke ghost
hardening into form,

fleshy knees and fists
marbled at the altar rail.
You're still the baby

who asked no deliverance.
We're not fallen.
We're great apes, pupae, whales,

you're a studious, overheated
ostrich, as unformed as
imagery in your mind's eye,

fortune's adolescent child,
daydreamer on the move.
Check out how you look to God.

11. By the Seawall

Broken rocks and concrete. Rammy waters.
Foam seeds, furls, starbursts and rosettes.
Granular spume blurs the air and falls.

The crows' dainty feet, tapping the stones,
don't alight long enough for me to write
the complete sentence that this is.

Veil and flail churn through their changes,
like changes of heart or mind, like will
switching its passion object to object.

What else? The spindled waters look like
old tight-waisted crinolines, petite, dressed
on dummies, puzzled why no body fills them out.

The voices of the dead, the soon-to-be, we children
of fortune, the unlucky and bereft, the unseen,
speaking all our appeals and sorrow.

I want my young body back, its small raucous jump.
The moment mourns itself. The sea calls us
to ourselves, to lives and things gone missing.

The swells and waves in their disorder
hold and hold, a perfect authenticity, like we
who still feel so immediate, dreamed up, and past.

The Playhouse Near Dark, Elizabeth Holmes
On the Vanishing of Large Creatures, Susan Hutton
One Season Behind, Sarah Rosenblatt
Indeed I Was Pleased with the World, Mary Ruefle
The Situation, John Skoyles

2008
The Grace of Necessity, Samuel Green
After West, James Harms
Anticipate the Coming Reservoir, John Hoppenthaler
Convertible Night, Flurry of Stones, Dzvinia Orlowsky
Parable Hunter, Ricardo Pau-Llosa
The Book of Sleep, Eleanor Stanford

2009
Divine Margins, Peter Cooley
Cultural Studies, Kevin A. González
Dear Apocalypse, K. A. Hays
Warhol-o-rama, Peter Oresick
Cave of the Yellow Volkswagen, Maureen Seaton
Group Portrait from Hell, David Schloss
Birdwatching in Wartime, Jeffrey Thomson

2010
The Diminishing House, Nicky Beer
A World Remembered, T. Alan Broughton
Say Sand, Daniel Coudriet
Knock Knock, Heather Hartley
In the Land We Imagined Ourselves, Jonathan Johnson
Selected Early Poems: 1958-1983, Greg Kuzma
The Other Life: Selected Poems, Herbert Scott
Admission, Jerry Williams

2011
Having a Little Talk with Capital P Poetry, Jim Daniels
Oz, Nancy Eimers
Working in Flour, Jeff Friedman
Scorpio Rising: Selected Poems, Richard Katrovas
The Politics, Benjamin Paloff
Copperhead, Rachel Richardson

2012
Now Make an Altar, Amy Beeder
Still Some Cake, James Cummins
Comet Scar, James Harms
Early Creatures, Native Gods, K. A. Hays
That Was Oasis, Michael McFee

Blue Rust, Joseph Millar
Spitshine, Anne Marie Rooney
Civil Twilight, Margot Schilpp

2013
Oregon, Henry Carlile
Selvage, Donna Johnson
At the Autopsy of Vaslav Nijinksy, Bridget Lowe
Silvertone, Dzvinia Orlowsky
Fibonacci Batman: New & Selected Poems (1991-2011), Maureen Seaton
When We Were Cherished, Eve Shelnutt
The Fortunate Era, Arthur Smith
Birds of the Air, David Yezzi

2014
Night Bus to the Afterlife, Peter Cooley
Alexandria, Jasmine Bailey
Dear Gravity, Gregory Djanikian
Pretenders, Jeff Friedman
How I Went Red, Maggie Glover
All That Might Be Done, Samuel Green
Man, Ricardo Pau-Llosa
The Wingless, Cecilia Llompart

2015
The Octopus Game, Nicky Beer
The Voices, Michael Dennis Browne
Domestic Garden, John Hoppenthaler
We Mammals in Hospitable Times, Jynne Dilling Martin
And His Orchestra, Benjamin Paloff
Know Thyself, Joyce Peseroff
cadabra, Dan Rosenberg
The Long Haul, Vern Rutsala
Bartram's Garden, Eleanor Stanford

2016
Something Sinister, Hayan Charara
The Spokes of Venus, Rebecca Morgan Frank
Adult Swim, Heather Hartley
Swastika into Lotus, Richard Katrovas
The Nomenclature of Small Things, Lynn Pedersen
Hundred-Year Wave, Rachel Richardson
Where Are We in This Story, Sarah Rosenblatt
Inside Job, John Skoyles
Suddenly It's Evening: Selected Poems, John Skoyles

2017
Disappeared, Jasmine V. Bailey
Custody of the Eyes, Kimberly Burwick
Dream of the Gone-From City, Barbara Edelman
Sometimes We're All Living in a Foreign Country, Rebecca Morgan Frank
Rowing with Wings, James Harms
Windthrow, K. A. Hays
We Were Once Here, Michael McFee
Kingdom, Joseph Millar
The Histories, Jason Whitmarsh

2018
World Without Finishing, Peter Cooley
May Is an Island, Jonathan Johnson
The End of Spectacle, Virginia Konchan
Big Windows, Lauren Moseley
Bad Harvest, Dzvinia Orlowsky
The Turning, Ricardo Pau-Llosa
Immortal Village, Kathryn Rhett
No Beautiful, Anne Marie Rooney
Last City, Brian Sneeden
Imaginal Marriage, Eleanor Stanford
Black Sea, David Yezzi

2019
The Complaints, W. S. Di Piero
Ordinary Chaos, Kimberly Kruge
Mad Tiny, Emily Pettit
Afterswarm, Margot Schilpp